PUNCTUM:

Wick Poetry Chapbook Series Five
Catherine Wing, Editor

Poppy Seeds · Allison Davis

Here Both Sweeter · Daniel Carter

I Left My Wings on a Chair · Karen Schubert

Determinant · Alex Fabrizio

Local Fauna · Brian Brodeur

Little Nest · Diana Lueptow

Seven Boxes for the Country After · Janet McAdams

Punctum: · Lesley Jenike

PUNCTUM:

Poems by Lesley Jenike

The Kent State University Press
Kent, Ohio

© 2017 by Lesley Jenike
All rights reserved
ISBN 978-1-60635-333-2
Manufactured in the United States of America

The Wick Poetry Series is sponsored in part by the Wick Poetry Center at Kent State University.

Cataloging information for this title is available at the Library of Congress.

"What I hide by my language my body utters."

—Roland Barthes

CONTENTS

ACKNOWLEDGMENTS

The Birmingham Poetry Review: "Splitting the Lark," "Twelfth Night"
Cave Wall: "The First Appeal"
Diode: "The Mirror Stage," "Walhalla"
The Gettysburg Review: "Practice," "The Beast"
Harpur Palate: "A Woman Gives Birth to Someone Who Won't Last"
Natural Bridge: "Punctum"
Passages North: "Proofs"
Tupelo Press Quarterly: "The Canon"
Waxwing: "Reading Whitman Postpartum"

THE CANON

That we'd seen a boy of twelve or thirteen riding a roan mare bareback through rye made no difference. We couldn't take the time to stop,

but if we had, we might've seen a whole village, its barn doors thrown open, all horses to market, each one young and sound. And in the air we'd smell the wholesome crush of dung and chimney smoke, and imagine the boy's other stock: a dapple grey colt he'll sell next month once it's broke. Stamping its hay, snuffling its grain, it smells the sweet tang of its own sweat. Sun through the stall's slats draws up the dust to which they—boy, roan, and grey—will go back.

Or we might've seen a high rise in Dublin where a boy tethered his horse to a stop sign. Next month he'll clatter it on blacktop down to Smithfield Market and sell it to a boy just like him: sweatpants, gym shoes, a yellow squirt gun. He belongs to a gang of kids whose ponies are called for rappers or favorite biscuit brands. They never need a saddle or bridle. What works is a fistful of mane, billy club tied to a belt with twine, mean-eyed looks, a wolf whistle. The market's cordoned streets will shine with piss and blood. Someone will be shot with a real gun and a horse will stagger from too little food onto cobblestone.

I'm waking up in the passenger seat and my father tells me how we nearly crashed, how he spun our rental's wheels toward a wall, dodging an oncoming tractor, a flock, a car, all while I was sleeping, my headphones on, and in my lap an upside-down, half-read book wherein a boy refuses to grow up, is forced to sell his horse, then dies alone—in a city or on a dirt road, it makes no difference to anyone.

PRACTICE

The nurse sighs, "I don't hear a heartbeat"
and we both look. On-screen: Henry James's term

made flesh—*ficelle*—coined to facilitate,
minor in character, held by ellipses.

For clarity, think of the drawing rooms
in *The Portrait of a Lady.* Male suitors

drift in liminal spaces, their own lives
thumbed-over pages, or the bad ghosts in

The Turn of the Screw, whose gravities we
can't sound—can't or don't want to. Think of art

vanished to loft fire or flood, no proof
it was ever made, blacked out then guessed

by future life studies. That's how this feels,
a tiny figure haloed like a thumb-

nail moon: the portrait of no likelihood. But
the doctor calls it "practice," snapping off

the screen, tearing up the spit-out photograph.
"Next time," she says, "it'll be the real thing."

PROOFS

In winter it's a lean snow that stacks itself. It's a dog of a snow
that grows its bent for drift and howls to stick. Look:

a man in a cranberry hoodie on Finley Street says, "Leave it!"
to his pit bull, and the pit bull leaves it.

On the causeway above the ravine, one schoolboy attempts to
prove to his friend that a feather will fall faster than a stone.
He's proven wrong, white goose feather in one hand, stone
from the creek in the other, when on count of three, he lets
them both go.

The stone of course plummets fastest while the feather—aping
its past as a bird—hovers, flutters, glides, and curls before it
lands, so much later than the stone, it's nearly spring—and
not yet spring.

A neighbor somewhere revs his motorbike, which sounds like
a backfiring gun, and the congregations that remain scatter
and take wing.

WALHALLA

Catalogued in leaves, first the wounding
heliotrope, next Walhalla's blood ravine,

highest level of existence, say the Vikings.
On the corner of Walhalla and Midgard,

a house for sale, advertised: *Not Haunted,*
looms its cupola like a ram's horn

in a god's hand. *Not haunted*—a double negative
on otherwise positive acreage, and where

Walhalla's light combs out the wood,
all our un-haunted houses on their hills

look down at their one road. *Not* haunted
like gazing the wrong way through binoculars,

to see smallness instead, and distance,
but how can we stop, through Walhalla's

phantasmagoria of October rot, our living
real estate's spectral impoverishment,

and what cost Walhalla if living so near
Heaven is living with its heavenly lack too,

non-ghost in the kitchen, non-ghost
on the stair, your honeyed roast in the oven,

your hot face in the bathroom mirror,
non-ghost, your non-child, swaddled in

the papered nursery, and if you look
past yourself you might see him there.

THE FIRST APPEAL

I slept first in a walk-in closet. Hung
and racked: my mother's sylvan backed

in cedar, ordered by season. Beyond
was her bedroom and beyond that the hall,

and beyond still a wooded corner lot.
I lay at the heart. Later, I had a window

over the lawn and old elm, its hard bark
I nicked my teeth on. As kids at a vacant

farmstead we called *Titanic* for its hulk,
snapped, bow to stern, by the roiling turf,

we'd hold each other up to look: red mold
at the crown molding, wood floors scraped

by so many chairs, dining room, living room—
grown-up worlds abandoned by grown-ups,

grown-up talk in all its smoke gone now
from the inglenook, pasture in flowering

weed, paddock ripe with mud and scat
and all we need do was jimmy the lock.

REALTY

"Life is sculpting me. Let it finish its work."
  —*Orpheus*, 1950

is a bungalow, backyard gone to seed
with a busted wooden platform nailed
to a dead tree some neighbor kid crawls up,
judging by the little rotten ladder,
slanted and enchanting, leaned against the trunk.
A *liability*, our agent says.
If you buy this place, tear it down. We'd hoped

the cape cod with its hornet's nest pendant
like a cruel locket above the door, its drive
buckling and taxable acreage
your daddy would die mowing, he said, might
bring you back, a homing blip against the black
of perpetuity. Owning is hell,
but see, I couldn't bring your notion

to term with a shared bearing wall, sex sounds
groaned around by neighbors in showers, spats,
and bad singing seeping by the decibel
into our bedroom to rankle us there.
No wonder I failed, as if I'd stepped over
a window frame a fellow renter tossed
behind our duplex, not through it, into

that private square of broken glass and grass
and splintered paint. I'd looked behind myself
to see if you were there, and saw moves
by the year-full, awful place after place,
every staircase too tight for a box spring,
and your waning baby face, back and back
to ether: a mortgage, I think, will bring you here.

TWELFTH NIGHT

We'd planned it for months: *Twelfth Night* on the lawn in a park named for a German poet. We'd spread our blankets on one bard's grass to hear another bard's language, all copasetic in the symmetry of

me being pregnant, my friend being pregnant too, someone bringing the sangrias with overripe fruit, someone else his rescue mutt and guacamole, someone else still the cookie bars and Diet Coke.

But it was summertime and the ether rough. Back in early April we couldn't know what would happen, that June would give way to July, that the ocean would give back torrents to the earth, that I wouldn't be pregnant anymore, but she would.

On the day of, we texted one another, watching the sky bloom storms to wither them to bloom them again: "r u still coming," we asked. Our answers were mixed, but most of us showed,

the stage manager standing on the raised platform looking up, the shipwreck set souring in the on-again, off-again rain, and the twins backstage, ready for the squall to tear them apart.

THE MIRROR STAGE

In a final fête of pain, earth scars itself
with Indian pipe and crabapple, carapaces

of reverse tenderness, and like a girl pleading
to crueler things: an arrant hand, those trees.

The biggest welt of all as seen from above
is our little river. Beside it, at a reclaimed lot

just south of town, we watch an employee
of the Audubon Center bend down, his hands

in latex, bundling a dead wren in a blossom
of paper towel. The windows there that face

the water are stuck with spasms of stickers
shaped like birds as seen through tear blur,

meant to stop birds from flying into glass: birds
into birds: but they do by the misery every year.

THE HAWK

My stepfather held the hawk in a towel
and it died in his arms. How many times
have we thought he'd do the same in ours?
Not that we could hold him—he's too big, too old.
A neighbor girl, my mom said, stood watch,
came into her kitchen, and helped her cook
ground beef for the hawk. She was thrilled to think
the hawk might live, but it didn't.
After my stepfather got his new liver
he shook over the letter he wrote
in his carpenter's script to the mother
whose son died so he could live. He crumpled
every draft of it and wept. I once spent
a month in the state where he was born,
and sent back an ancient Vermont barn
on a postcard: a trite sign of collapse,
the kind that drives us deeper into woods,
and when we creep back at last it's the mind
resigning itself. We could try and save
the hawk but fail. What would the trying help?
The neighbor girl held a hawk that night
in her dream. It had smashed against a window.
She was a doctor and performed the deft
removal of its heart set like quartz
in a watch, then woke in time to place it
in her baby brother's open chest, this
gift she's giving him of wind, blood, and wing.

SPLITTING THE LARK

"Nature is a haunted house—but Art—is a house that tries to be
haunted."
  —Emily Dickinson

because everything's explicable—
the little mountains, the little river,
the woods for all their sinister mushroom
and fern, the bones of a lark so hollowed
by design no one need look. But look now,

we're splitting apart. We find our song
by sliding on headphones, by logging on
to databases and choosing the bird
by shape to hear its voice delivered
electronically like faith. In the breach

where the fulcrum was, in place of the hinge
is the nothing I was worried about,
the nothing to close the door, the nothing
to open it, the nothing to swivel
the sky near: its clouds above us props

in a lark about wombs or locks.
                                We drowse
in cattails and listen: purple martins
speaking honeyed garbage, flocks as from
a sand dollar spilling into the hand
that split it. We think we can hear our lost

baby, now a grade-schooler, chance sovereign
of the falls, exultant as I hold him
over the rocks, and like a jackdaw gab
his native talk—all words run together
in a nonsense pot of lush syllables—

then he's gone again. Ours is a haunted house
that shifts on its axis, and we're back
at the start, walking childless to the river
where it falls. But no, it's not the house, not
the dozer by the dig. It's not the falls.

It's our language: what can we call a thing
that *is* and *is not*—that gush of feeling
we stand-in for *river,* the feeling of
having let drop the *gold* in *goldenrod,*
till what's left but the sting and spring of blood?

A MOTHER GIVES BIRTH TO SOMEONE WHO WON'T LAST

With thanks to Fanny Howe

Morning come the inevitable separation:
a body from its sheet, finch from its perch
on our car's side mirror. You're like the sun
up from a crouch under Prospect Hill
sliding the rickrack curtains open
and the sad lab past a stand of trees breaks
from sleep to start his morning sob, a sigh
to part the vapors. A mob of Harleys,
in for their annual rally, crack
the pavement and practically split the air
in half. Time is a lake, upstate New York,
and its personage on Earth that biker's girl
at Lanzi's by the Dock, who said last night,
loud enough so we all could hear, "I hate
to even mention *him,* but it's so much
smoother riding with *you.*" Her current man,
his face long and brown, turned to the water
and took a drag off his cigarette, its smoke
freeing itself, satisfied by her show of faith,
it seemed. You put your hand on my belly
to shield the baby who isn't here yet, but
to the *now* man, the *smooth-riding* man,
smoke is a good death. There's no running from it.

"THE SUN IS GOD"

—J. M.W. Turner's last words

Of a sudden we're in the mortal classroom
and time drones on. Breath, water, and why what

must surface must, pain lectures at us
from a sweat-and-blood-smeared backcloth. Then sun

during its lesson about this world slips
behind a veil and you're born. What's clear is

he could look all he chose at the ocean
from his Brighton boarding room,

but Turner needed to walk the chalk hills
with his paints and canvas, to feel the yolk

slide between his fingers and into it.
To be washed by that hardtack tear into something

evanescent like a god on his tongue,
he must know the sea can't be just blue stone,

or a puddle, or a smudged glass of water,
but a palm open to welcome the sun.

ST. FRANCIS AND THE NEWBORN

At sixteen my life just fit my body

like a fist of white thrift fits a pitcher.

But I wanted to give it back, to back

away from it and run. Or sleep heavy

in it, taking up every spare room.

    We'd taken the bus from Rome. Our guide said,

    Take an hour then meet us by the church

    at noon. I chose to nap in a park, day-

    pack snug under my skull, under the day-

    pack, earth. And I dreamt I was an aspen

    with white bark white sheets of bark and a crush

    of birds, my trunk too lean to house them. Bells,

    crowds at the vestry. I woke up covered in wings.

        So the self shifts to make more room,

some of me still there in Assisi,

some of me with you here in your room,

you suckling, and I'm stretched tight like the rind

of a balloon—milk, more milk. The body

is ceaseless, seeks to assist. So much was

empty before you came. I was crouching

somewhere in my right hand, huddled. The rest: air.

THE BEAST

You speak to her in English, but English
deliberate in its mouthfeel, like cake
from the vegan bakery: modified
for illusion's sake, made broader somehow
by its vegetable parallel. Many

syllables are best for learning and lolling
on the animal fat of your tongue, so
civilization. We can choose to feed
egg and amaranth to the baby, need
and resistance to need: the human mix

you let tumble between daddy babble—
kimchi, honeycomb, relish—
words pressed in a grist sweetened by us,
her makers, who are both soft and hard
depending. We can be enlightened if

the bodily hunger outgrows itself.
And they say it will. But her open mouth
spirals to stars, sings for pith in yowls
so sharp it scares you. Her face is
your face. I'm somewhere deeper in.

READING WHITMAN POSTPARTUM

"A child said *What is the grass?* fetching it to me with full hands"

It's wild love elsewise mowed by the young
and sleeveless. It's play catch. It makes dull thuds.
Its blades are among us, and having died
as he lived—in the grass—it's fodder for
our dead dog and Berber in the great room,
umbrage for those whose brick courtyards tousle
in wind and twinkle with cricket and matchstick,
with bottle cap and tick, a harmonium
of spit thread and leaf droning among the slabs,
calling all faithful to lay down and make do.

He Who Would Not Change Diapers carried me
on his back as he cut the grass, they say.
Now my daughter, resplendent on her eighth-
month blanket, with an arm like a slow crane,
scoops then lifts to the waiting garden of
her mouth the loose fringe and change for compost.
If we let her swallow, a lawn will grow;
it's the pulped guts of grassland beasts left
in the sun to make photographs. It's more
of a good thing and of course it's less.
It's rot begging with small hands to enter
the mall, the Auto Zone, the Venice
of our old neighborhoods, mooring the bee
that bobs at their docks. It's spangled night
in grey scale, till morning wet with drool.

It's the cool floor of a tent pitched. It's go
fetch and hurry, turn russet. It's waiting,
stultified under snow. It's slow cartwheels
then who knows—calling her in for supper
only to find a different pair of shoes,
scuffed and grassy, kicked off in a hurry
by the door, and her voice calling for you.

PUNCTUM

The names of their makers are on the bottoms of some brown paper bags. I hadn't noticed that before.

Brown paper bags aren't generally as strong as they once were. The weight of them, the heft—good for bringing home heavy electrical equipment, bottles of beer, or milk—like many things over the years, has diminished.

This bag was made by Maribel, it says. Maribel, wherever you are, in my first ever yoga class, I held a woman up by a strap and she didn't cry, then I let her hold me up by a strap and I didn't cry. I stood behind her body and while I was there I simply concentrated on lifting her hips, because for some reason this practice—the lifting of another person's hips by a strap—brings us nearer to health and happiness. There are things in this life I'll never understand.

Maribel, when you crafted your paper bag, did you consider what it would carry, all the many things it might someday carry?

We're linked beyond the bag that at this moment doesn't hold anything, is folded on a shelf in the hallway that leads down to the basement, though I fear my telling you might suggest what you've made isn't fine and it is fine.

Maribel, we're linked beyond the bag you made. I'm myself a vessel as is every woman no matter her will to carry or to not carry as are you, your name stamped on the underside of the paper bag like an insect in process, the hard black outline of you, letters squashed into a new state of being—from crawling to winged.

In a stray moment of boredom I turned the bag over once the eggs, the apples, the magnum of wine had categorically been put away, and I saw what I'd done, what I'd missed. This is Barthes's punctum, as Nabokov says, "that little sob in the spine," the thousand-page novel condensed to just one image: my hands turning over the paper bag to see your name there, my hands ripping the bag as I lie on my back on the green lawn, my hands ripping the bag slowly so I can see its woof of fibers detach and its insides, so I see between its two halves the sky.

Maribel, it's like looking through a stand of woods.

As I stood behind the woman, holding her up by a strap, I looked down at my hands, how in gripping they whitened, their blood running where—who knows—and I was a girl on horseback again, the field gilded, chasing an imaginary fox, my hands bound by leather and my mare's mane. A light touch, a light touch, I told myself then, easy and light as the hem of a long dress trailing over the sobbing grass, Maribel.